3/97

Justices of the Supreme Court

LOUIS
BRANDEIS

The People's Justice

Suzanne Freedman

ENSLOW PUBLISHERS, INC.

44 Fadem Road	P.O. Box 38
Box 699	Aldershot
Springfield, N.J. 07081	Hants GU12 6BP
U.S.A.	U.K.

Dedication

To the memory of Jerome Freedman, who was my best friend and strongest supporter. He would have been happy that I got on with my life.

Library of Congress Cataloging-in-Publication Data

Freedman, Suzanne, 1932—
    Louis Brandeis: the people's justice / Suzanne Freedman.
        p. cm. — (Justices of the Supreme Court)
    Includes bibliographical references and index.
    Summary: Includes the use of anecdotes to present the personal and
professional life of the first Jew to serve on the Supreme Court.
    ISBN 0-89490-678-X
    1. Brandeis, Louis Dembitz, 1856–1941—Juvenile literature.
2. Judges—United States—Biography—Juvenile literature. 3. United States. Supreme
Court—Biography—Juvenile literature. [1. Brandeis, Louis Dembitz, 1856-1941.
2. United States. Supreme Court—Biography. 3. Judges. 4. Jews—Biography.]
I. Title. II. Series.
KF8745.B67F74   1996
347.73'2634—dc20
[B]
[347.3073534]
[B]   95-24503
                                        CIP
                                        AC

Printed in the United States of America.

10 9 8 7 6 5 4 3 2 1

Photo Credits: Boston Public Library Research Library Office, p. 40; Brandeis University Special Collections Department, pp. 9, 35, 38; Collection of the Supreme Court of the United States, pp. 13, 18, 68; Franklin Delano Roosevelt Library, pp. 29, 53, 71; Harris & Ewing, Collection of the Supreme Court of the United States, pp. 46, 56, 65, 75; Library of Congress, p. 50, 61; Suzanne Freedman, pp. 27, 77, 83; University of Louisville Archives & Records Center, pp. 20, 22.

Cover Photo: Portrait by Eben F. Comins, Collection of the Supreme Court of the United States.

921
BRANDEIS
1996

 CONTENTS

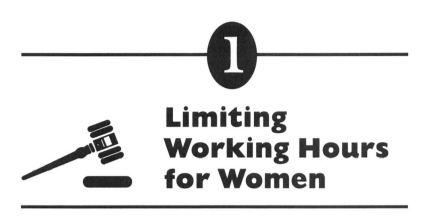

Limiting Working Hours for Women

Out of the ashes of the Civil War (1861–1865) arose a booming industrial America. The postwar period was a time when huge companies employed tens of thousands of workers. Companies such as the American Tobacco Company and Bethlehem Steel were founded. These companies, and dozens of others like them, demanded men and women work longer and longer hours in the factories, often for low wages. There were few laws limiting the hours that these laborers could work. Workers had no choice but to keep working, trying to make ends meet for their families. Organizations such as the National Consumer's League waged battles in the courts trying to pass laws regulating work hours and wages. The American Federation of Labor (AFL), an organized union of workers with almost two million members, also tried to improve wages for its members. Even Theodore Roosevelt, the President of the United States, sought social reform to correct the abuses and injustices that workers suffered at the hands of businesses that had become too big.

Limiting Working Hours

State laws limiting working hours were consistently ruled unconstitutional by the United States Supreme Court. In 1905, for example, the Court struck down a New York law limiting the hours male bakery employees could work as "an infringement of the liberty of contract without due process of law."[1] Associate Justice Rufus W. Peckham wrote the majority opinion in *Lochner* v. *New York*:

> Clean and wholesome bread does not depend upon whether the baker works ten hours per day or only sixty hours a week. . . . We think that there can be no fair doubt that the trade of a baker . . . is not an unhealthy one to that degree which would authorize the legislature to interfere with the right of labor. (If the Court upheld this law) no trade, no occupation, no mode of earning one's living could escape this . . . power.[2]

Two years after the *Lochner* ruling, however, gender and a persuasive lawyer would succeed in swaying the High Court. After the *Lochner* case, employers challenged every state law restricting work hours. Oregon passed a law "limiting women's work in manufacturing and mechanical establishments and laundries to no more than ten hours a day."[3] The Oregon authorities charged Curt Muller's Grand Laundry in Portland with breaking the law by requiring Mrs. Elmer Gotcher to work longer hours. Muller was convicted and fined ten dollars for the offense. Muller appealed his conviction to the Oregon

Supreme Court. When it upheld the conviction, Muller brought his case to the United States Supreme Court. He claimed that the Oregon law violated his right to "liberty of contract" as implied in the Fourteenth Amendment to the Constitution of the United States:

> No State shall make or enforce any law which shall abridge the privileges . . . of citizens of the United States; nor shall any State deprive any person of life, liberty, or property, without due process of law. . . . [4]

An organization of women known as the National Consumers League heard about the Muller case. The National Consumers League, organized in 1899, drafted laws regulating hours, wages, and working conditions. The Consumers League label stitched on a manufacturer's product meant that state factory laws were obeyed by the company, goods were made on the premises, no overtime was required, and children under sixteen were not employed. The league's director and guiding influence, Florence Kelley, stepped in and immediately enlisted the aid of her trusted advisor and close associate, Josephine Goldmark. When the two women heard that Muller would appeal to the United States Supreme Court, they set out to fund the finest legal talent in the country to defend the Oregon law. First, they called on a well-known New York attorney, Joseph H. Choate. But Choate said he saw no reason why "a big husky Irishwoman should not work more than ten hours a day in a laundry if she and her employer so desired."[5]

Goldmark then thought of her brother-in-law, Louis Brandeis. Kelley and Goldmark hurried up to Boston to meet with Brandeis in the library of his home. Brandeis had represented many clients without charging a fee and was known throughout Massachusetts as "the people's lawyer." He agreed at once to take the case without charging a fee. This case was right up his alley: a test of a constitutional issue concerned with the welfare of the "little guy" in an industrial society. Brandeis would have preferred that workers' hours be decided by employers and unions. But unions were not yet strong enough in 1908 to negotiate successfully for working conditions. He thought that both men's and women's work hours should be limited. The Supreme Court had ignored this argument when it struck down the New York law in *Lochner.* "Maximum hours statutes might be constitutional," the Court had declared, "where the state demonstrated that specific injury to the workers could result from overwork."[6]

So Brandeis decided that the best tactic would be to focus on women, pointing out their particular health problems caused by long working hours. Because of the Court's past ruling, Brandeis knew the only way to be convincing was to overwhelm the Justices with a lot of statistics and to present enough facts to make the Court believe the "welfare of the weaker sex lay in their hands."[7] He sent Goldmark to find "facts, published by anyone with expert knowledge of industry in its relation to women's hours of labor . . . factory inspectors, physicians, trade unions, economists, social workers."[8] With the aid of ten "readers," Goldmark combed the libraries of Columbia University, the New York Public Library, and the Library of Congress in Washington, D.C. Evidence had to be gathered to show that females suffered under strain from overwork, that fatigue added to chronic ailments and accidents, and that shorter hours would result in economic and social benefits.

Louis Dembitz Brandeis at his desk. He was known throughout Massachusetts as "the people's lawyer."

The Brandeis Brief

The Brandeis Brief, as it would come to be known, was uncommon for its time in that it departed from the usual style. It contained only two pages of traditional legal arguments. There was a ninety-five page section entitled "The World's Experience upon which the Legislation Limiting the Hours of Labor for Women is Based,"[9] and fifteen pages of state and foreign laws that limited women's working hours: The laws in nineteen states and seven European countries contained restrictions, in one form or another, on the hours of labor that could be required of women. There were over ninety reports of committees, bureaus of statistics, commissioners of hygiene, and factory inspectors in the United States and abroad who stated that long working hours are dangerous for women.

One such inspector from Hanover, Germany, summed it up:

> The reasons for the reduction of the working day to ten hours—(a) the physical organization of women, (b) her maternal functions, (c) the rearing and education of the children, (d) the maintenance of the home—are all so important and so far reaching that the need for such reduction need hardly be discussed.[10]

"It was the attorney's duty," Brandeis said, "to bring courts the facts available to the legislature, which was the . . . information judges had to have if they were to make the right decision."[11] Brandeis presented his oral argument before the Supreme Court in *Muller* v. *Oregon* on January 15, 1908. Associate Justices Edward D. White, Rufus W. Peckham, William R. Day, Joseph McKenna, Oliver Wendell Holmes, William H. Moody, John Marshall Harlan, and David Josiah Brewer sat on a raised platform behind a railing on either side of Chief Justice Melville A. Fuller, who occupied the center chair. Brandeis stood in front of the Justices in an area ringed by wooden benches for spectators.

Brandeis thought of oral argument as a work of art, and he was a master.

> A proper statement of a case, is like a pebble dropped into a still pond from which widening concentric circles [circles having a common center] flowed outward. The point where it entered the water was the first statement made to the Court; each of the circles a statement of fact complete in itself, raising no question in the hearer's mind, satisfying it, occupying it wholly. . . . The first sentence should tell the Court what kind of a case is before it.[12]

Brandeis, at fifty-two, looked younger than his years. ". . . His smooth face square and strong. . . . His eyes twinkle behind his nose glasses . . . a large frame, but sparingly filled out . . . his voice is soft and drawling, but it can snap like a whip lash. . . . when he began to talk his face [lit] up with intense interest." Admirers compared him to Abraham Lincoln. One observer noted "[He had] a large head, . . . stubborn black hair streaked with iron gray . . . sensitive hands . . . of a musician. . . . All in all, [he] gave one . . . an impression of originality and power."[13]

Brandeis began to address the Justices: "We submit . . . it cannot be said that the Legislature of Oregon had no reasonable ground for believing that the public health, safety, or welfare did not require a legal limitation of women's work in manufacturing and mechanical establishments and laundries to ten hours in one day."[14] Brandeis listened to William D. Fenton, counsel for Muller, argue that "Women, equally with men, are endowed with the fundamental and inalienable rights of liberty and property, and these rights cannot be impaired or destroyed by legislative action under the pretense of exercising the police power of the state. Difference in sex alone does not justify the destruction or impairment of these rights."[15]

After the Justices listened to both sides, they met to discuss the case. Nearly six weeks passed before the announcement came. The Court had upheld the Oregon statute in a 9-0 decision.

In writing the unanimous opinion, Justice Brewer mentioned Brandeis by name: "In the brief filed by Mr. Louis D. Brandeis," he declared, "is a very copious collection of all these matters. . . ." (It was unusual to mention an attorney by name in a Court opinion, but Brandeis's factual approach had never before been attempted.) Brewer continued:

> Woman's physical structure and the performance of maternal functions place her at a disadvantage in the struggle for subsistence. . . . [H]ealthy mothers are essential to vigorous offspring. . . . [T]he limitations which this statute places upon . . . her right to agree with her employer as to the time she shall labor, are not imposed solely for her benefit, but . . . for the benefit of all. . . . [T]he two sexes differ in structure of body, in the functions to be performed by each, in the amount of physical strength, in the capacity for long-continued labor, particularly when done standing, the influence of vigorous health upon the future well-being of the race, the self-reliance which enables one to assert full rights, and in the capacity to maintain the struggle for subsistence. . . . [W]e are of the opinion that it cannot be adjudged that the act in question is in conflict with the . . . Constitution, so far as it respects the work of a female in a laundry, and the judgment of the Supreme Court of Oregon is affirmed.[16]

Brandeis's factual approach forced the Supreme Court to rethink its usual stand that the Constitution was unchanging. He was one of the first lawyers to base his case not on legal argument, but on facts and statistics.

Brandeis had won his case. He had convinced the Supreme Court to depart from its usual stand that the Constitution could not be changed. He had represented the rights of women workers everywhere. He had set a precedent for "bringing into the courtroom the kind of information that reflected what was really going on in the world outside."[17]

Josephine Goldmark would recall in later years that the:

> . . . distinguishing mark of . . . Brandeis's argument was his complete mastery of the details of his subject and the [gathering] of evidence. Slowly, deliberately, without seeming to refer to a note, he built up his case from the particular to the general, describing conditions authoritatively reported, turning the pages of history . . . all to prove the evil of long hours and the benefit that accrued when these were abolished by law.[18]

The entire legal profession was electrified. Brandeis's argument in the Muller case, the Brandeis Brief, had become a model for future lawyers. Requests for copies poured into the National Consumers' League, which reprinted the brief and the decision. The state of Illinois reenacted maximum-hour laws for women that the Court had struck down in 1895. Similar laws were passed in Virginia, Louisiana, and Michigan and in 1912 in Ohio, Washington, and California. Attorneys in other cases began to use the Brandeis Brief. At the Harvard Law School, Professor Felix Frankfurter, a future Supreme Court Justice, told his students this was an epoch-making technique. Some years later, Louis Brandeis was asked what he would call this collection of facts gathered to support the idea that women are different from men. Brandeis came right to the point. He replied, "What Any Fool Knows."[19]

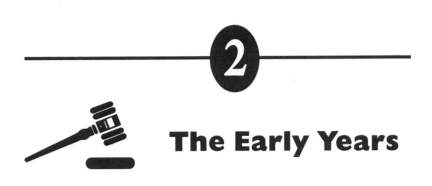

The Early Years

German-Jewish immigrants Adolf and Frederika Brandeis came from Prague (capital of what is now the Czech Republic) in 1848 to seek political freedom in the United States. The Midwest was full of opportunities for the free-spirited couple. Adolf and Frederika spoke only German. They settled in Ohio, but their dream of starting a farm colony there was soon abandoned. They decided to move to Madison, Indiana, a town of ten thousand people, which is midway between Cincinnati, Ohio, and Louisville, Kentucky. Adolf became convinced that the best opportunities were in the great river traffic of the Ohio River.

River traffic was heavy in 1848. The development of passenger and freight steamboats had reached its height in the decade from 1840 to 1850. Passenger steamboats were "veritable palaces for their time."[1]

Madison contained the station of the Indianapolis and Madison Railroad, the first to be built in Indiana. The railroad ran eighty-six miles, from Madison to Indianapolis, and supplied central Indiana with sugar, rice, coffee, and molasses, which were then carried north by steamer from Madison. The railroad also brought back Indiana farm products for distribution downriver to towns like New Orleans in Louisiana. Madison was a good place to live in the 1840s. It was a pleasant setting and there were promising opportunities for work.

Adolf decided to build a factory in Madison. He also opened a grocery and produce business. Adolf had a little experience working in a grocery store in Cincinnati, which proved invaluable during the two years he had the factory. The factory failed, but the grocery and produce business grew. Adolf would travel either by horse and buggy or on horseback to buy butter, eggs, and vegetables. In this way, he could expand his knowledge of the country and its resources while getting to know the people who lived along the Ohio River.

There were over half a million German people and a million Irish people in the United States in 1860.[2] But Germans outnumbered other immigrants in the Ohio Valley. The German language was widely spoken. Often, English-speaking residents learned to speak German. Abraham Lincoln, driving his buggy through the fifteen counties of the Eighth Judicial Circuit, where he tried law cases, "carried a German grammar [book] and studied the language in a night class."[3]

The country grew between 1850 and 1860. The gold rush in California was over, manufacturing was growing in the North, and the Mexican War had ended. Texas had been admitted to the Union in 1845. The great West with its vast expanse had captured the imagination of many European immigrants.

In 1853, Adolf and Frederika moved with a partner to Louisville, Kentucky, to develop a wholesale grain and produce business. The young company, which they named Brandeis and Crawford, gradually expanded to include river traffic as far south as New Orleans. They eventually ran a flour mill, a tobacco factory, an eleven-hundred-acre farm, and their own freighter, *Fanny Brandeis*, named after the eldest of their four children, who was born in 1851 in Madison. Amy, Alfred, and Louis were born after the family moved to Louisville. Louis, born on November 13, 1856, grew up playing on the docks of the Ohio River. River captains were his heroes.

Louisville in the 1850s was a "large and flourishing town."[4] Into this thriving community, in a little house on Center Street, Louis David Brandeis was born. Louis, the youngest of four children, had a normal childhood.

The whole area around Louisville was swampy and Louis and Alfred had frequent mild bouts of malaria. Malaria, a disease caused by infectious mosquitoes, left them feeling run-down. Louis was devoted to his brother, Alfred, who was two years older. Louis and Alfred remained close for the rest of their lives. "My heart rejoices," Frederika wrote to Louis years later, "when I see you [and Alfred] happy together. . . . [T]here were never two brothers who complemented one another so perfectly and were so completely one as you two."[5]

Brandeis's Childhood

Louis was only five years old when the Civil War began. "I remember helping my mother carry out food and coffee to

Louis Brandeis was the youngest of four children. He was especially close to his brother, Alfred.

the men from the North. The streets seemed full of them always. But [t]here were times when the rebels came so near we could hear the firing."[6]

Like his sisters and brother, Louis was given every educational advantage. He attended Miss Wood's private school, the German and English Academy of Louisville, and the Louisville Male High School. When he was sixteen years old, Louis was awarded a gold medal by the Public Schools of Louisville for his excellent work.

The Brandeis family was a close-knit group: idealistic, intellectual, and self-reliant. The most dominating figure of this group by far was Louis's uncle and namesake Lewis Dembitz. Louis would later change his middle name from David to Dembitz in his honor.

The Brandeis family were abolitionists, people opposed to slavery. They had servants, but they were never treated as slaves. From both his parents, Louis inherited sound judgment, faith in humankind, and a sense of community pride and civic duty.

The Brandeis family was Jewish, but did not belong to a synagogue. The children were brought up without any formal Jewish training. Louis's mother taught her children that religion went hand in hand with basic moral virtues. She believed it had nothing to do with rituals. Louis shared his mother's belief.

After the Civil War ended in 1865, the United States experienced a period of great wealth. Eight years later, however, the nation plunged into a depression and did not recover until 1879. During the depression many businesses failed. The firm of Brandeis and Crawford suffered heavy business losses. Many of their southern clients had businesses that also failed. Not wanting to risk any more losses in the

19

This is the building where Louis spent most of his days as a young boy.

economic crash they saw coming, the firm was dissolved. Adolf would wait for better times to start a new business. He decided to take the family to Europe to visit relatives and stay until the economy improved in the United States. In the spring of 1872, the Brandeis family left Louisville.

The Brandeis family stayed in Europe for two years. Louis wrote in his journal:

> This experience had for me . . . the greatest advantages and I have attributed my own attitude toward money and life . . . to the fortunate circumstances of my father's troubles in a way. As a boy, I had everything that money could buy . . . but in the important years of my life—age 13 and 14 and up to the time I became independent, I had to pass through the experience of having practically nothing.[7]

High School Years

The years abroad deepened Louis's Americanism. Schooling in Germany meant far more to him than the usual routine of subjects. In the fall of 1873, Louis decided to enter the Annen-Realschule, a high school in Dresden, Germany. His family could not go with him because Fanny and Amy were still very ill with typhoid fever in Switzerland. The seventeen-year-old boy was to get a taste of independence by making the trip to Dresden alone. For the first time, he had to use his own resources. When he arrived at the school he managed to gather up the courage to enter the principal's office. The principal stated flatly that he could not be admitted without taking the entrance exam and submitting birth and vaccination certificates. Louis was willing to provide proof of a vaccination by inviting the principal to look at his arm. His presence certainly was evidence enough that he had been

MALE HIGH SCHOOL.

LOUISVILLE, KY.

Report of *L. D. Brandeis*

In Recitation, Deportment and Attendance for the Scholastic Year 1871-2.

REPORT		No. 1	No. 2	No. 3	No. 4	No. 5	No. 6	No. 7
Belles Lettres,	6	6	6	5.7	6	6	6	5
Latin,	5.5	5	5.8	5.4	5	5.8	6	6
Greek,	5.4	5	5.9	6	6	5	6	6
Pure Mathematics,	5.9	5.7	6.0	6.0	5.7	5.9	6	6
Applied Mathematics,	—	—	—	—	—	—	—	—
Chemistry and Technology,	6	6	5.5	6	6	6	6	6
French,	5.3	5.95	6	6	6	6	6	6
German,	5.4.58	5.90	5.7	5.9	6	6	5.8	5.8
Total Rank in Study,		5.96	5.88			5.96	5.97	
No. Demerits,		—	—	—	—	—	—	—
Deportment,		6	6	6	6	6	6	6
General Class Standing,		5.98	5.94				5.95	5
No. Times Absent,		—	—	—	—	—	—	—

EXPLANATION.—Deportment is determined by the number of Demerits received, regarding 100 as 0, and none as 6. General Class Standing is determined by adding Rank in Study to Deportment and dividing by 2.

SCALE OF AVERAGES.—0, signifies failure; 1, very bad; 2, bad; 3, indifferent; 4, good; 5, excellent; 6, without fault.

Parents and Guardians will please indorse each Report, and return it.

Wm McDonald _____ Principal.

This report card from Louis's sophomore year at Louisville Male High School shows his excellent marks. He would eventually finish his high-school training at Annen-Realschule in Dresden, Germany.

born. He argued his case so successfully that the principal allowed him to enter the school without taking the required exam. Louis Brandeis was showing early powers of persuasion.

His grades rarely changed in the three terms Louis attended the Annen-Realschule. They ranged from *gut* ("good") to *sehr gut* ("very good"). His subjects included French, Latin, German, literature, mineralogy, physics, chemistry, and math: "although [I] did well in [my] studies theretofore," Brandeis later recalled, "it was not until [I] went to Dresden that [I] really learned to think . . . in preparing an essay on a subject about which [I] had known nothing, it dawned on [me] that ideas could be evolved by reflecting on your material. This was a new discovery for [me]."[8]

Louis became increasingly annoyed at the inflexible aspects of faculty-student relationships. One night, for instance, he returned to school at a late hour. Discovering that he had forgotten his key, he began to whistle loud enough to wake up his roommate. He was scolded by a stern schoolmaster. "This made me homesick," he said. "In Kentucky you could whistle! I wanted to go back to America and I wanted to study law. My uncle . . . was a lawyer; and to me nothing else seemed really worthwhile."[9] When his parents decided to return home in the spring of 1875, Louis couldn't wait to go with them. While visiting friends in Brookline, Massachusetts, Louis made plans to enter Harvard Law School in Cambridge that fall.

Harvard Law School

Not yet nineteen, with no formal college training and a few hundred borrowed dollars, Louis Brandeis entered Harvard Law School on September 27, 1875. He had prepared for his new studies just by reading Kent's *Commentaries on American Law* that summer. "My thoughts are almost entirely occupied by the law . . . ," he wrote. "Law schools are splendid institutions."[10] Harvard Law School's two hundred students attended classes taught by a dozen or so faculty members in a two-story brick building known as Dane Hall. Courses such as contracts, property, civil procedure, criminal law, evidence, trusts, and constitutional law were offered. There were also law clubs where students could argue cases for practice. Brandeis's years at Harvard were among the happiest of his life.

Graduation from Law School

In the spring of 1877, after what was then the required two years of law school, Brandeis was ready to graduate. He had earned the highest grades in his class. At graduation, six men had to be selected to write a speech; the man who would deliver it was to be selected by the faculty. Louis, who was then twenty years old, led the class in the popular vote. The rules of Harvard University, however, stated that no one could graduate who was not twenty-one, and the faculty had to abide by them, but the speaker had to receive his degree before he turned twenty-one. The question came up: How could a man who was not twenty-one be the speaker when he couldn't even receive a degree? Dean Christopher Columbus Langdell was troubled.[11] He really wanted Brandeis to deliver the speech. He pondered and thought and stroked his beard but he couldn't do anything about it. Finally, he sent Louis to President Eliot who said, "The rule is that the orator is to be one of those who receive a degree before . . . twenty-one. You won't be twenty-one until November [of the next academic year]. Commencement is in June [of this academic year]. I don't see, Mr. Brandeis, how you can be the orator." Brandeis thought, "There is an example of an efficient executive."[12] Actually, Brandeis was relieved. Writing a speech was a lot of work, and he was contemplating spending an extra year to take a postgraduate course anyway. But on commencement morning, as a result of a special vote, he did receive his degree.

Louis Brandeis's years at Harvard were not completely easy. Aside from financial problems, he suffered from poor eyesight. In the years he attended law school, his father had just about managed to pay off his debts but was unable to pay Louis's tuition. After his brother Alfred's loans got him through the first year of law school, Louis applied for and was granted a scholarship. Also, one of his professors suggested he try tutoring, and by the beginning of the second year, it proved to be quite profitable.

Louis Brandeis went regularly to a nearby gym to keep in shape. He had weak muscles and a frail physique and was given a course of limited but regular exercises, which he never abandoned. Eyestrain, an ailment fairly common among law students of the day, continued to bother him. He would read constantly under the flickering lights of an old gas lamp. These were the days before electricity, televisions, and stereos. His eyes began to give out after the first year of law school, and that summer he consulted several specialists. The trouble was muscular, they said, and prescribed eye exercises. Another doctor told Brandeis to abandon his chosen career. But this was something he would never do. "One mistress only claims me," Brandeis wrote in his notebook. "The 'law' has her grip on me and I suppose I cannot escape her clutches."[13]

". . . It won't hurt you to read less and think more,"[14] yet another specialist advised. So, Brandeis decided to find fellow

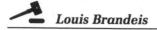

students to read to him. That way, he would be forced to use his already sharp mind and to store up legal principles in his head. One of the students who read to Brandeis was Samuel Warren, the son of a wealthy paper manufacturer. Their close relationship led them to eventually become law partners.

Opening a Law Practice

In the summer of 1879, Warren and Brandeis hung out their shingle at 60 Devonshire Street, "a desirable location . . . in the 3rd story (2 flights). . . . The room (no. 5) . . . only $200 a year—very cheap. . . ."[15] The partners hired a messenger boy for three dollars a week. The firm picked up business quickly. In January 1880, Warren and Brandeis began gaining many new clients, including a successful paper manufacturer from New Hampshire and a steamship company.

At the same time, Brandeis began clerking for Chief Justice Horace Gray of the Massachusetts Supreme Judicial Court at a salary of about $500 a year. Most of the work was done in the summer months and did not interfere with his private clients. "I consider Brandeis the most ingenious and most original lawyer I ever met, and he and his partner are among the most promising law firms we have got," said Justice Gray.[16]

Marriage

Brandeis returned to Louisville for a sad occasion on March 5, 1890. His oldest sister, Fannie, had died at the age of thirty-nine. At the funeral home he met his second cousin, Alice Goldmark, from New York City. They had many common interests: a love of literature and culture as well as similar ideas. Their serious interest in each other grew. They fell in

Louis Brandeis and Samuel Warren opened a law office together in
Boston. Brandeis's desk now sits in the Brandeis Room of the
Judaica and Special Collections departments at Brandeis University.

love. On March 23, 1891, they were married by Alice's brother-in-law, Felix Adler.

Alice was not very strong physically and had difficulty handling everyday affairs. She left it to Louis to arrange for house repairs and to deal with electricity and heat and water problems. The house Louis purchased on Mt. Vernon Street was next door to close friends. It had a center hall, a reception and dining room, a library, and three bedrooms. The Brandeises managed to live simply but well. Louis Brandeis was determined to become financially independent as early as possible, but he had no intention of killing himself to become rich. Sufficient rest and frequent vacations were always part of his routine. He gave his family a fair share of each day: Susan, the eldest of Louis and Alice's two daughters, born on February 27, 1893, and Elizabeth, born three years later on April 25, always ate a seven o'clock breakfast with their father as soon as they were old enough. After breakfast they would read together for an hour. He would arrive at his office regularly at about 8:30 A.M. The office contained just a desk and chairs—no rug or easy chair. He would dispose of his mail by 10:00 A.M. When he saw clients, the conference would be quick. Brandeis usually sat quietly and listened intently to what his client had to say. Quickly, with just a simple comment or question, he would get to the heart of the problem. Brandeis ended the business day promptly at five o'clock and went horseback riding or, weather permitting, canoeing on the Charles River.

Brandeis took a vacation whenever he needed one, usually in August. "I soon learned that I could do twelve months' work in eleven months, but not in twelve,"[17] he used to say. One August was spent in the Canadian wilderness, sailing,

At the end of a long day and on vacation, Brandeis enjoyed canoeing. He is shown here canoeing on the Potomac River in Washington, D.C., in 1919.

fishing, walking, canoeing, and mountain climbing. This trip and others like it gave him time to think, reflect, and unwind.

By the year 1890, Brandeis had become a successful corporation lawyer, earning about $50,000 a year. He dealt only with leaders of big businesses as his personal clients and never acted as a legal employee of the company itself. He preferred to have clients rather than to be a corporate lawyer. Well-known Massachusetts manufacturers became clients as well as his lifelong friends. Brandeis refused to serve a client when the person acted improperly. If he thought one of his clients was wrong, Brandeis would advise him to admit his error and settle out of court.

Nothing, however, was more important to Brandeis than the process of education. In 1924, after serving as a Supreme Court Justice for eight years, Brandeis started donating books and papers to the Louisville Law School and continued to do so until the time of his death, on October 22, 1941. Alice died four years later. It was Louis and Alice's wish to be cremated and have their remains buried at the entrance to the law school.

Louis Brandeis's high sense of moral obligation and his dedication to public welfare were due in large part to his parents, Adolf and Frederika. He concluded early on in his legal career that public involvement was important. Not only did he have a successful law practice in Boston, but he became recognized across the country as "the people's lawyer."

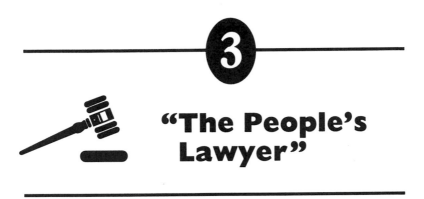

3

"The People's Lawyer"

In the 1880s, during Brandeis's early years as a lawyer, a revolutionary age was beginning in the United States. Land was being absorbed, the wide-open spaces of the frontier were closing. Farming was no longer the center of American life. New industries sprang up. Huge mills and factories produced iron, steel, and copper. Local slaughterhouses were replaced by meat-packing plants, and companies like General Mills supplied grains to the growing urban populations. Mines were opened to provide fuel for factories. Millions of people from all over the world came to the United States to work in the factories, mills, and mines. People moved from rural to urban areas, and big businesses were taking over. They increasingly replaced the earlier family-owned businesses.

As industries grew bigger in the 1800s, the corporation became more common. It would eventually become the leading form of business organization in the country. In order to start a corporation, interested parties have to apply to a state legislature for a license to start a particular business. Once given a license, or charter, the interested persons can then organize a corporation and sell shares of stock, or certificates of ownership, to raise the money needed to carry on the business. Those who invest their money are called stockholders or shareholders.

These corporations were owned by a handful of people. In the mid-1800s, businessmen needed increasing amounts of money to build, equip, and operate new manufacturing businesses. Because the corporation was ideal for gathering large amounts of money, it came to be widely accepted. During the last half of the 1800s, there was a growing trend toward business combination. Corporations in similar businesses joined together to create large combinations. In that way, they could save money by eliminating competing salesmen and advertising and by dealing as one with transportation companies, workers, and banks.

Monopolies

These large corporations ran the risk of becoming a threat to important principles of people's freedom. If a group of corporations combined, they might gain a monopoly, or complete control over a particular line of business. Monopoly control could dry up the flow of competition, which is at the heart of free enterprise.

Other businessmen developed another form of business consolidation known as a trust. In order to organize a trust you first had to reach an agreement with the major leaders and investors in a corporation. Under a trust agreement, the promoters of the trust gained control of the corporation itself. In exchange, the promoters or trustees gave the investors trust certificates. The investors then made a profit on the trust.

During the 1870s and 1880s giant trusts swallowed up corporations in many of the country's big industries, including oil, steel, sugar refining, and whiskey distilling. This new spirit of fierce competition made people work at a faster pace. Even though it was an exciting time, some of the changes created problems. Many Americans had to adjust to a new way of life.

A general progressive reform movement promoting regulation of big business began to take shape by the early 1900s. Progressive reformers, and Brandeis was certainly one, worked for honest and efficient government and a democratic system that would benefit everyone. Progressivism was a revolt of the middle classes—small businessmen, editors, professors, clergymen, and other professional groups—against a system where huge companies dominated the economy and political life of the nation. The progressives disliked the change from the conditions they had known. Brandeis declared, "Nearly every American boy could look forward to becoming independent as a farmer or mechanic, in business or professional life. . . . Today most American boys . . . believe that throughout life they will work in some capacity as employees of others."[1]

Low-Cost Transportation in Boston

Brandeis and the progressives tried to stop the power of these new industrial tycoons and the negative side of industry and to promote a return to an earlier and better society. Brandeis's first major effort as a progressive reformer came in 1897. Brandeis's law firm became known as Brandeis, Dunbar and

Nutter (Sam Warren had left to take over his family business). The interests of Brandeis's varied clients in his private practice helped him learn more about Massachusetts issues and politics. He became involved in a fight on behalf of the public. At that time, the population of Boston had grown to over half a million, an increase of over 25 percent in ten years. The city had no public transportation system, only trolley lines operated by private companies. There was a lot of congestion in downtown Boston. Eventually, a subway was built and leased to the West End Railway, a privately owned company. In 1897 the Boston Elevated Railway, another private company, got the rights to operate "at fares not below five cents for the next thirty years."[2] The company was trying to gain control over Boston's transportation system. Opposition grew. Brandeis represented the Board of Trade, which was made up of local merchants who had an interest in low-cost transportation.

The fight against the Boston Elevated Railway was an early example of Brandeis's legal technique. He sent out letters trying to get support from prominent citizens, lawmakers, and friendly journalists. His method was to get the facts to the people and to urge them to get after their lawmakers. Brandeis believed that education and democracy went hand in hand. The fight was successful. The city of Boston had managed to keep control of its transportation system.

The Board of Trade thanked Brandeis, who had represented it without a fee. Brandeis liked being a "free man who could donate his labor to public service."[3]

Regular Hours of Employment

In 1896, Brandeis was to get a closer look at the relationship between work and money. One of his clients, William

34

Louis Brandeis (center) believed that education and democracy go hand in hand. Working for the Board of Trade, local merchants who had an interest in low-cost transportation, he educated Boston citizens on the dangers of a monopoly. His efforts, and those of concerned citizens, defeated the Boston Elevated Railway.

McElwain, a Massachusetts shoe manufacturer, was having a hard time. His employees refused to accept a cut in salary and went on strike. McElwain called in Brandeis for advice and was told that, although his business was in a slump, his employees had been earning unusually high wages and were working under good conditions. Brandeis visited the shoe plant and learned that the employees' work was seasonal. There were many days when there was no work to be done at all. McElwain said the average wage earned was high. "I abhor averages," said Brandeis. "A man may have six meals one day and none the next, making an average of three per day, but that is not a good way to live."[4] Brandeis then spoke with the head of the International Boot and Shoe Union, who was acting as the striking workers' representative. He wanted the employees' wages calculated on the basis of time worked. McElwain wanted to pay them according to how many pairs of shoes they produced. Brandeis rejected both proposals and suggested that the work could be spread out during the year. He advised McElwain to get orders far enough in advance to provide work throughout the year. McElwain agreed. The factory was then able to operate 305 days each year, and wages were substantial and regular. Both employer and employees benefited.

Savings Bank Life Insurance

Brandeis always considered Savings Bank Life Insurance (SBLI) one of his most important achievements. He did not think that the "Big Three" insurance companies: Metropolitan of New York, Hancock of Massachusetts, and Prudential of New Jersey were well run. He was first introduced to the life insurance system in 1905. Almost immediately, he began to read the reports of various life insurance companies to learn more about the subject. He soon discovered there were no legal safeguards to protect those people who bought insurance policies as there were for savings bank depositors. Brandeis collected facts and took home "suitcases filled with reports from insurance and banking companies."[5] He began to compare life insurance companies to savings banks and discovered that the life insurance companies lacked proper management.

Brandeis supported an idea that appealed to other reformers: Savings banks should open insurance departments. Depositors would find it easy to buy insurance from banks they trusted. On March 21, 1907, the Joint Legislative Committee of Massachusetts held hearings on Brandeis's plan. The Committee voted for it 10-4. The bill was then sent to the state's House Ways and Means Committee, where it was debated and voted upon. On June 26, 1907, Massachusetts governor Curtis Guild signed the bill. It took a year to implement it. Finally, the Whitman Savings Bank sold its first insurance policy to Charles Henry Jones, a Boston shoe manufacturer. On November 2, 1908, the People's Savings Bank of Brockton, Massachusetts, opened its first insurance department. Savings Bank Life Insurance (SBLI) was in business. By 1912, thirteen Massachusetts savings banks had become insurance agencies, thanks largely to the efforts of Louis Brandeis. Today, life insurance is offered "over the counter" in mutual savings banks in three states—Massachusetts, New York, and Connecticut. Massachusetts has the oldest plan in operation (1908), then New York (1939), and Connecticut (1942).

Railroad Monopolies

The New Haven Railroad, which already dominated New England's transportation system, wanted control of the

In 1908, Louis Brandeis founded Savings Bank Life Insurance. He considered it to be one of his most important achievements.

Boston & Maine Railroad (B&M). If the merger went through, it would create a monopoly. Brandeis was hired by a major B&M investor to fight the takeover by New Haven. He declared war against the New Haven, a battle that began in 1905. Brandeis decided that since this was a matter of public interest, he could not accept a legal fee. Large corporations, he said, "threatened the political as well as the economic well-being of the community."[6]

After much research, Brandeis published a pamphlet exposing New Haven Railroad's financial losses, due to shabby accounting practices, showing that the real purpose of the merger was to cover its losses. The pamphlet created a lot of excitement.

Eventually, the Interstate Commerce Commission (ICC) began its own investigation of the New Haven Railroad. Every one of Brandeis's charges was verified. The ICC discovered that the line had not made essential track and equipment repairs, the negligence resulting in a sharp rise in accidents. New Haven stock dropped. The New Haven Railroad was ruined.

Brandeis became involved in other labor disputes, and he got to know union leaders firsthand. "I am experiencing a growing conviction that the labor men are the most congenial company," he wrote his brother, Alfred, after resolving a strike; "labor unions should strive to make labor share all the earnings of a business except what is required for capital and management."[7]

The New York garment workers went on strike in 1910. Nearly sixty thousand workers, most of whom were Eastern European Jewish immigrants, worked in crowded conditions, crammed into tenements, facing low wages, long working hours, and a life of endless labor and economic insecurity.

This political cartoon from the February 15, 1911 *Boston Post* demonstrates that all the railroads in Boston wanted Brandeis on their side.

They insisted they would not return to work until the manufacturers recognized their demands, agreed to them, and accepted a "closed shop." A closed shop is a business in which the employer hires only union members in good standing. A labor union is an organization concerned with job improvements for its members. A union negotiates wages, hours, working conditions, and job security. It also arranges labor contracts and handles job disputes.

Brandeis was called in to help. He eventually worked out an agreement that included minimum wages, maximum hours, holidays, a joint Board of Sanitary Control to monitor working conditions, committees to fix piecework rates, and a system for the settlement of disputes. While working out the settlement during the day, he spent the evening hours relaxing with the employees' negotiating committee. He found them intelligent and eloquent and open to democratic procedures. They would talk to Brandeis about the anti-Semitism (prejudice against Jews) they had experienced in Europe and the United States. For the first time in his life, Brandeis began to face the problem of anti-Semitism.

Zionism

Louis Brandeis's family never seemed to consider it important that they were Jewish. They did not practice the Jewish religion—or any religion, for that matter. Why then did Brandeis become involved in Zionism? Perhaps his close relationship with his uncle and mentor, Lewis Dembitz, was an important influence. Settling the Garment Workers' strike and getting to know Jewish workers from Eastern Europe played a big role as well. A meeting with Zionist leader Jacob de Haas, on August 13, 1912, was probably the most

41

important factor. De Haas, editor of Boston's *Jewish Advocate*, "unfolded the Zionist cause to Brandeis, ". . . a movement to give the Jews . . . the land of their fathers where the Jewish life may be lived normally and naturally, and where [they] can govern themselves. . . ."[8]

The idea of a Jewish state did not sit well with some American Jews who wanted to be thought of as Americans first.

What really promoted the Zionist movement in the United States was Brandeis's "persona and mystique, his charm, fluency, sincerity and passion, the thrill of being part of a movement that he headed."[9] Jacob de Haas described Brandeis as "a Jew who is keen to feel and think with his people and, who the world over, has come to be known as Israel's greatest spiritual guide and most practical adviser . . . whose private office . . . is a temple to which men and women make pilgrimages from all the ends of the earth."[10] Brandeis was so well known that when he appeared at annual Zionist conventions, the audience would rise to their feet. They looked upon him as a prophet (someone who predicts events) and pledged their devotion and faithfulness.

Brandeis's national reputation was now firmly established. In 1912 and 1916, he would find a receptive and supportive audience in Democratic President Woodrow Wilson.

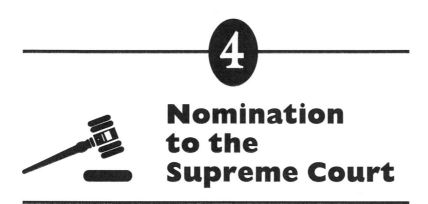

4

Nomination to the Supreme Court

Woodrow Wilson, who taught political science at Bryn Mawr College, Wesleyan University, and Princeton University, later became president of Princeton University from 1902 to 1910. By 1910 he had established a national reputation as a strong supporter of democracy. He was offered and accepted the Democratic nomination for governor of New Jersey, and was elected easily. Two years later he became the Democratic party's hope for the presidency. Brandeis called Wilson's nomination "among the most encouraging events in American History."[1] Brandeis did not know Wilson well, but Wilson knew Brandeis as one of the spokesmen for the Progressive Movement.

Adviser to President Wilson

When President Wilson seemed uncertain, he would turn to his informal adviser Louis Brandeis. In April 1914, Brandeis proposed the establishment of a federal trade commission that would regulate business. After a hard battle, Wilson won a decisive victory—the Federal Trade Commission Act was passed on September 26. The new law committed the federal government to a policy of strong regulation of all business activities and outlawed unfair trade practices.

Wilson used Brandeis's suggestion for the fundamental issue of his presidential campaign—that labor and business should be free of monopolistic control. Wilson promised to destroy monopolies and to restore conditions under which competition could grow. He would accomplish this by freeing credit from Wall Street control and outlawing unfair trade practices. This program, called the New Freedom, stressed individual enterprise and social and economic justice. Wilson said:

> I take my stand absolutely, where every progressive ought to take his stand, on the proposition that private monopoly is indefensible and intolerable. And there I will fight my battle. . . . I am for big business, and I am against trusts. Any man who can survive by his brains, any man who can put the others out of business by making the thing cheaper to the consumer at the same time that he is increasing its intrinsic value and quality, I take off my hat and say: "You are the man who can build up the United States, and I wish there were more of you. . . ."[2]

"Vote for Roosevelt, pray for Taft, but bet on Wilson!" was one voter's opinion on how to vote the election of 1912.[3] Wilson won a landslide victory with 435 electoral votes and more than 6 million popular votes over Progressive party candidate Theodore Roosevelt and old guard Republican William Howard Taft.[4] Wilson became the nation's twenty-eighth president and only the second Democrat to be elected president since the Civil War.

Once the election was over, Wilson's first task was to select a team of advisers. Speculation increased as to Wilson's choice for attorney general. There was a lot of talk about Brandeis. Brandeis had achieved a certain status as a trusted adviser to the president and other law makers. But Wilson did not offer him the position. Local party bosses had been important to Wilson's election, and he thought it best not to anger them. Brandeis was "too controversial . . . too antagonistic . . . perhaps the American most hated by big business, financial leaders, and the railroad interests[;] . . . I simply could not appoint a radical. . . . [The attorney general] cannot be a person of the crusader type in public life," Wilson said.[5] He appointed James Clark McReynolds instead. Brandeis sent a congratulatory message to the new attorney general.

Another presidential election was taking shape in the background in 1916. Wilson, running for a second term, was confronted with a reunited Republican party. Republicans stood firmly behind their candidate, Supreme Court Justice Charles Evans Hughes. In the closest presidential election in history, Wilson got 277 electoral votes to 254 for Hughes. Wilson gained 49.4 percent of the popular vote, and Hughes got 46.2 percent.[6]

Brandeis owed a great deal to Wilson, who had given him the opportunity to put some of his economic ideas into effect. Brandeis, on the other hand, was an invaluable adviser to the president. In addition to giving fully of his time and energy to the Federal Reserve Act, Brandeis gave comments, criticisms, and suggestions to Wilson about another important bill in 1914, which became law as the Clayton Antitrust Act. The

Although President Wilson did not appoint Brandeis attorney general, he did value Brandeis as one of his most trusted advisors.

act prohibited businesses from selling at lower prices to certain favored purchasers if it helped to create a monopoly. The act also declared that strikes, peaceful picketing, and boycotts—three ways of expressing disapproval over working conditions—were legal. It was a clear-cut victory for organized labor, who referred to the act as their Charter of Freedom.

Brandeis's access to the president and his cabinet also helped him gain support for the creation of a Jewish homeland, his chief goal as a Zionist. President Wilson, although he had failed in his first term to appoint Brandeis as attorney general, nominated Brandeis to the Supreme Court in 1916. Brandeis's confirmation, however, was not achieved without a long and bitter fight.

Nomination to the Highest Court in the Land

When Supreme Court Justice Joseph R. Lamar died on January 2, 1916, everyone in Washington was talking about who would succeed him. Since Justice Lamar had come from Georgia many assumed that he would be replaced by a southerner. Massachusetts was already represented by Justice Oliver Wendell Holmes. Former president William Howard Taft wanted the job, too. Wilson talked with Treasury Secretary William Gibbs McAdoo and Attorney General T.W. (Tom) Gregory about nominating Brandeis. Gregory praised Brandeis but warned Wilson against the nomination. Wilson asked Wisconsin Republican senator Robert "Bob" LaFollette whether progressive Republicans in the Senate would vote to confirm Brandeis, a Democrat. LaFollette enthusiastically said yes. Samuel Gompers, the powerful labor leader, was also consulted, and Wilson received strong assurance of labor support for the Brandeis nomination. The only person left to consult with was Louis Brandeis himself. On January 24, Wilson sent United States attorney George W. Anderson to meet Brandeis in Bridgeport, Connecticut, to offer him the nomination. After careful consideration, Brandeis accepted. "I am not entirely sure," he wrote his brother, "that I am to be congratulated but I am glad the President wanted to make the appointment and I am convinced . . . that I ought to accept."[7]

Brandeis was almost sixty years old at the time. He was still vigorous and active, but he could not keep up the physical pace he had been used to. His wife, Alice, was concerned that he pushed himself too much. A position on the Supreme Court might just be the answer. Alice wrote her brother-in-law Alfred, ". . . I tell Louis, if he is going to retire, he is certainly doing it with a burst of fireworks."[8] Louis wrote Alfred: ". . . I should have preferred to be let alone until sixty-five."[9] Brandeis knew that as a Supreme Court Justice his freedom of action for public causes would be limited, but like Alice, he thought a Court seat would be good for his "retirement" years.

The Confirmation Process

The fireworks began exploding four days after the announcement of Brandeis's nomination and continued to explode for six months. Just after noon on January 28, 1916, a clerk delivered a short message from the White House stating, "To the Senate of the United States, I nominate Louis D. Brandeis of Massachusetts to be Associate Justice of the Supreme Court of the United States."[10] Ever since President George Washington had nominated someone to the Senate, requests had been granted with very little fuss. But this announcement resulted in an uproar. Mainly the issue was whether or not to admit a social reformer and highly political individual into the conservative world of government law.

Conservatives were in shock. Some people felt that the very fact that Brandeis was Jewish was sufficient reason to "bar him from the Temple of the law."[11] Senator John D. Works, a California Republican, summed up his displeasure with Brandeis's appointment by saying, "He [Brandeis] seems to like to do startling things and work under cover. . . . He is of the material that makes good advocates, reformers, and crusaders, but not good or safe judges."[12] On the other hand, Brandeis supporters felt he was the kind of man the Court needed, a liberal and a reformer—"a prophet of humane law."[13] A friend wrote former president William Howard Taft, "When Brandeis's nomination came in . . . the Senate simply gasped. . . . [T]here wasn't any more excitement in the Capitol when Congress passed the Spanish War Resolution."[14]

The Brandeis nomination was about to become one of the most controversial in the history of the Supreme Court.

On January 31, within three days after Wilson nominated Brandeis, a five-member Senate subcommittee was established. News reporters, witnesses, and a few staff members attended, but Brandeis, the nominee, did not attend. Senator William Edwin Chilton, a fifty-eight-year-old Democrat from West Virginia, was the chairman of the subcommittee. Next to him sat Senator Duncan Fletcher of Florida, the second Democrat on the subcommittee and a man more interested in the "price of farm products than in passing on the merits of federal judges."[15] At fifty-six, the youngest and third Democrat was Thomas J. Walsh of Montana. Albert Baird Cummins and John Works represented the Republican side. The progressive Cummins

As this political cartoon indicates, Brandeis's appointment to the Supreme Court shocked many conservatives.

was close to Senator Robert LaFollette, an ardent Brandeis supporter.

Newspaper articles repeatedly noted that Brandeis's being Jewish was an advantage, because senators would not want to be labeled anti-Semitic if they did not approve his nomination. Only one other Jew had been proposed for the Supreme Court seat: in 1850 President Millard Fillmore had offered the position to Judah P. Benjamin of Louisiana, who turned it down. Brandeis's entire career would be given a thorough examination. A Boston newspaper labeled him "radical, impractical, reckless, not possessing a judicial temperament that would fit him for the duties of the Supreme Court."[16] Attorney General Gregory suggested that Brandeis leave Washington while the hearings were proceeding; Brandeis agreed and returned to Boston and his law practice. Publicly, he refused to comment. When a *New York Sun* reporter inquired about the charges made against him, Brandeis would only reply, ". . . I have nothing to say . . . and that goes for all time and to all newspapers, including both the *Sun* and the moon."[17]

In Boston, he maintained silence. Letters for and against the appointment came pouring in. Charles William Eliot, former president of Harvard, wrote the committee that the rejection of Brandeis "would be a grave misfortune for the whole legal profession, the Court, all American business, and the country."[18] To which Brandeis's law partner McClennen replied, "Next to a letter from God we have got the best."[19]

On February 11, Harvard president A. Lawrence Lowell circulated a petition containing the names of fifty-five Bostonians: "We do not believe that Mr. Brandeis has the . . . capacity which should be required in a judge of the Supreme Court."[20] Another letter against the Brandeis nomination was sent to the subcommittee by seven of the sixteen former presidents of the American Bar Association, headed by William Howard Taft. The main charges were Brandeis's well-known sympathy for labor and his radicalism. Someone even suggested that Brandeis give up the fight for a Supreme Court seat and run instead for the Senate from Massachusetts against Henry Cabot Lodge. Lodge had encouraged the American Bar Association to oppose the nomination. President Wilson continued to maintain his support, stating that Brandeis "is a friend of all just men and a lover of the right; and he knows more than how to talk about the right, he knows how to set it forward in the face of its enemies."[21]

Over seven hundred Harvard Law School students supported Brandeis. Pro-Brandeis mail from union members all around the country began pouring into the White House. Of the more than six hundred letters received from Massachusetts lawyers, only eight were negative.

What angered Bostonians was that Brandeis, a Harvard Law School graduate who had given every indication of becoming a corporate lawyer, had broken away to be a reformer—and the target of those reforms had been Boston's social and economic elite. Louis Brandeis had made too many waves.

Brandeis now began to fight and fight hard. His many supporters moved from apathy to action. He enlisted the aid of Gregory, Bob LaFollette, and his old friend, Harvard Law School professor Felix Frankfurter, who wrote unsigned editorials to the *New Republic* urging confirmation. Other hard-hitting editorials began appearing in *Harper's Weekly*. Florence Kelley of the National Consumers League wrote to *Survey*. The *New York World* had supported Brandeis since the days of the life insurance investigation and continued to

Louis Brandeis (right) and Harvard Law School professor and future Supreme Court Justice Felix Frankfurter were old friends. Frankfurter urged Brandeis's Supreme Court confirmation in unsigned editorials in the *New Republic*.

back him. The managing editor of the *Independent* had worked with Brandeis on the Garment Workers' Strike and remained an ardent ally.

On April 3, Chairman Chilton announced that the subcommittee had approved the Brandeis nomination. The vote: three Democrats (Chilton, Fletcher, Walsh) against two Republicans (Cummins, Works). Now the nomination had to go to the full Senate Judiciary Committee of ten Democrats and eight Republicans. The outcome was still doubtful. Two defections from the Democrats could prove fatal. Both sides acted to delay through most of April. The matter hung in limbo. Brandeis grew angrier. He knew that Congress would come to a formal close of their session before the Republican National Convention on June 7. On May 8, Wilson wrote the committee members, urging them to act swiftly. The president had made it perfectly clear that he wanted this nomination approved.

Six days later, it still seemed that the votes of Democratic senators Hoke Smith of Georgia and Jim Reed of Missouri might be the deciding factor. On May 14, journalist Norman Hapgood, a Brandeis friend and supporter, invited Smith and Reed to have a drink at his apartment in Washington. Brandeis suddenly appeared and talked to the senators for over an hour, persuading them to vote for him.

On Wednesday morning, May 24, the Judiciary Committee voted for confirmation on a strict party vote, 10-8. It was now up to the Senate as a whole to decide. At 5:30 P.M. that same day, Vice President Thomas R. Marshall, presiding over the Senate, announced that Louis D. Brandeis had been confirmed as an Associate Justice of the Supreme Court by a vote of 47 to 22. All of the Democrats had voted for Wilson's nominee except for the senator from Nevada. All of the Republicans had voted against him except for LaFollette and two other senators.

At about the same time, Brandeis was leaving his Boston law office to catch the early evening train to his summer home. As he opened the front door, he was greeted by Alice with the good news. "Good evening, Mr. Justice Brandeis," she exclaimed.[22]

Four days later, in Washington, D.C., Brandeis rode to the old Senate Chamber in the Capitol from the Lafayette Hotel, accompanied by Chief Justice Edward Douglas White, who was to administer the oath of office. Among the many spectators in the packed courtroom were members of the Senate and House, government officials, and other close friends. In the reserved section sat Alice Brandeis, daughters Susan and Elizabeth, and brother Alfred. A large crowd stood in line waiting to be admitted.

Chief Justice White entered the chamber. The marble busts of former Chief Justices Roger Brooke Taney, Samuel Chase, Morrison Waite, and Melville Fuller looked down on this new moment of transition. The lean, slightly graying robed figure filed in last. Brandeis raised his hand and repeated the oath of office:

> I, Louis D. Brandeis, do solemnly swear that I will administer justice without respect to persons, and do equal right to the poor and to the rich, and that I will faithfully and impartially discharge and perform all the duties incumbent upon me as Associate Justice of the Supreme Court of the United States, according to the best of my abilities and understanding, agreeable to the Constitution and the laws of the United States. So help me God.[23]

Both Louis Dembitz Brandeis (back row, left) and John Hessin Clarke (back row, right) were appointed to the Court in 1916.

The first progressive Justice to be appointed to the Supreme Court took his seat on the bench at the beginning of the new term in October of 1916. Mr. Justice Louis Dembitz Brandeis, lawyer and public-spirited citizen, would now have a new forum from which to speak with even greater prestige. In the twenty-three years he served on the Court, he would chart a new course for Court decisions.

Brandeis on the Supreme Court

The Brandeis's apartment overflowed with papers and books, and the bathtub was filled with folders and clippings which might one day become useful in a Court case. Brandeis was as demanding of his law clerks as he was of himself. His clerks would spend long hours researching in libraries. If he needed to refer to a particular reference book, Brandeis, who had a photographic memory, would tell one of his law clerks exactly where to find it. One clerk remembered Brandeis making sixty changes in one opinion of ten pages, with some of his opinions going through maybe twenty or thirty versions. Brandeis delivered his opinions from the bench without referring to a single note. He had memorized them much as he had done during his law school days, when he had trouble with his eyes.

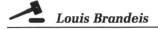

Justice Brandeis

The clerk would check in with Brandeis every morning, but set his own hours. Brandeis used the clerk's time with him to further the clerk's education; after all, he hoped each clerk would turn out to be a future law professor. One of his first law clerks was Dean Acheson, who would become secretary of state under President Harry S. Truman. After Acheson began his second year clerking for Brandeis, someone asked him to describe his boss: "he is one of the faithful," a "friend of the people . . . an enthusiast . . . [He] is the 'Plumed Knight.'"[1]

Justice Brandeis worked long and hard but he insisted that "it be with a fresh mind and at top efficiency."[2] As soon as he felt tired, he would stop working and stretch out on the couch in his study for a twenty-minute nap. Work would begin on the Monday morning following the Saturday conference of the Court. There the Chief Justice would hand Brandeis an assignment notice, a paper on which were written the docket numbers of cases assigned to him for an opinion. The Saturday conference began at noon. (Today, the conference takes place on Fridays, usually beginning at 10:00 A.M.) If the conference lasted past 5:00 P.M., Justice Brandeis would protest. Rising from his chair, he would say, "Chief Justice, your jurisdiction has now expired and Mrs. Brandeis's has begun."[3] He would then leave for home.

From the assignment paper, Brandeis would indicate to his law clerk the cases that he would start drafting and the ones the clerk would work on. He drafted in longhand. When a fair copy (a neat, exact copy) was needed, it was made by the court printer. This was no easy task because the original copy was very hard to read and put together with scissors and paste. The final proof was then circulated among the other Justices for editing, suggestions, and agreement or disagreement.

Louis Brandeis was a dedicated, hard-working Justice, but he made sure he also spent time with his wife, Alice. Here, they are traveling around Washington, D.C., in a horse and buggy in 1919.

Brandeis always tried to make the case before him as concrete as possible and to develop fully all the facts involved.

Brandeis on the bench was the prime example of a new Justice in action. In his first term, Brandeis wrote more than twenty opinions as spokesman for the Court and dissented five times. This was a pattern he would follow through all his years on the bench. _New York Central Railroad_ v. _Winfield_ was the first case to "focus the professional spotlight on him."[4] The case involved injury compensation to railroad employees working in more than one state. Brandeis argued that Congress, in passing the Federal Employers Liability Act in 1908, did give states power to provide protection needed for injured railroad workers. Relevant and easily available information exposed far-reaching abuses: extortion (pressure and intimidation), discrimination, misrepresentation, fee-splitting, and many other wrongs against workers. From the high bench of the Court, Brandeis could speak with authority. His minority opinions often carried greater weight than those of the majority. Brandeis's beliefs were reflected in the many opinions he wrote during the twenty-three years he served on the Supreme Court. Brandeis usually was in favor of four things: (1) action by individual states rather than by the federal government, (2) balancing corporations with unions, (3) encouraging business competition, and (4) experimenting with laws to help workers.

These positions are reflected in his dissent in a 1917 case shortly after he joined the Court. In _Hitchman Coal and Coke Co._ v. _Mitchell,_ he criticized the Court for upholding contracts that allowed companies to force their employees to agree not to join unions. He dissented in _Quaker City Cab Co._ v. _Pennsylvania_ in 1928 when the Court overturned a state law taxing corporations more than individually owned businesses and partnerships.

Another dissent in 1933, in *Liggett* v. *Lee,* attacked the Court for overturning a state law imposing heavier license fees on chain stores than on independent shops. In *Myers* v. *United States* in 1927, Brandeis again dissented; this time the Court allowed the president of the United States to fire a civil servant even though there had to be approval from the Senate for such a dismissal.

Brandeis decided with the Court whenever it struck down what he felt was a level of governmental assumption of power that was not in the Constitution or was inconsistent with democracy. He always insisted on maintaining the rights of the individual and the ability of all people to participate in the democratic process.

Brandeis tried to educate the judiciary and the public through his dissents and decisions. He sought to gather every bit of available information and filled these documents with facts and statistics to back up his arguments.

In the areas of labor relations and civil liberties Brandeis had deep differences with the majority of the conservatives on the court. In the 1921 case *Truax* v. *Corrigan,* Brandeis dissented, arguing that an injunction against picketing would prevent equality in labor-management relations. Concerned about individual freedom, he believed that the job of the federal government was to balance the forces of labor and capitalism in order to guarantee that freedom. He thought it legal and acceptable for labor to organize and protect the individual worker from the already powerful forces of big business.

Brandeis and Frankfurter

A Supreme Court Justice's work is a full-time job for anyone—but Brandeis did more. He advised five presidents: Warren Harding, Calvin Coolidge, Herbert Hoover, and most especially Woodrow Wilson and Franklin Roosevelt. He continued a second full-time career as a Zionist leader. He kept his interest in Savings Bank Life Insurance. He maintained an active involvement in Harvard Law School. One of the people Brandeis recommended as a Harvard Law faculty member was his friend and fellow graduate Felix Frankfurter. Brandeis had met Frankfurter in 1905 when Frankfurter, then a Harvard Law School student, heard Brandeis deliver a lecture at the Harvard Ethical Society in Boston. They became friends despite the great difference in their ages. Frankfurter was twenty-six years younger.

Neither one ran for public office, but preferred their roles as public/private citizens, which gave them more freedom to direct public policy. After Frankfurter served a brief stint as a law officer at the War Department in 1910, Brandeis urged him to leave government for the academic world. Frankfurter, however, wasn't sure he wanted to devote his life to teaching. After more consultations with his friends Oliver Wendell Holmes and Theodore Roosevelt, Frankfurter, at age thirty-one, decided to join the Harvard Law School faculty on September 1, 1914. He would continue teaching there for the next twenty-five years until he was appointed to the Supreme Court by President Franklin Roosevelt in 1939.

Brandeis and Frankfurter continued their close friendship, and by the time Brandeis joined the Supreme Court in 1916, he had absolute confidence in Frankfurter. Brandeis often described their relationship as "half brother-half son."[5] Throughout Brandeis's judicial career, he continued to discuss legal issues with Frankfurter, "trusting even the secrets of life on the Court to him."[6] And every year, Professor Frankfurter would select the most outstanding law school student to be

Both Oliver Wendell Holmes (left) and Louis Brandeis (right) encouraged Felix Frankfurter to leave government and join the academic world. Frankfurter listened to their advice and became a Harvard Law School professor.

Brandeis's law clerk, and Brandeis would accept the young man sight unseen.

When Chief Justice Edward Douglass White died on May 19, 1921, President Warren G. Harding appointed William Howard Taft to fill his place. It was a position Taft found entirely suited to his wishes, his temperament, and his abilities; it had been his lifelong ambition to be Chief Justice.

Taft and Brandeis had clashed five years earlier when Taft drafted a letter opposing Brandeis's nomination to the Court. Taft and Brandeis never allowed their personal differences to interfere with the Court's work though, and they would serve together on the bench for nine years. One rainy evening, shortly after Taft's appointment, Taft met Brandeis hurrying home for his punctual seven o'clock dinner. Taft grabbed Brandeis's hand and said, "I once did you a great injustice, Mr. Brandeis, I am sorry." Brandeis replied, "Thank you, Mr. Taft."[7]

The conferences of the Court had grown to be exhausting in the early part of 1921. Justice James Clark McReynolds, difficult at best, did not try to hide his personal dislike for the other two Wilson appointees, John H. Clarke and Louis Brandeis. McReynolds would not speak to Brandeis for the first few years they served on the Court together; nor would he visit homes where Brandeis had been invited. He even refused to be seated next to Brandeis where he belonged on the basis of seniority for the official Supreme Court photograph in 1924 (therefore, no picture was taken that year). He was bitterly disagreeable about Brandeis's opinions and would rise and leave the conference room whenever Brandeis began to speak.

Justice Oliver Wendell Holmes lived about a block away from Brandeis, and the two would walk together regularly.

"Brandeis's optimism and moral certainty . . . were cheering,"[8] Holmes would remark, and add, "Brandeis always has had the happy word that lifts one's heart. It came from knowledge, experience, courage and the high way in which he has always taken life."[9] Brandeis's former law partner, Sam Warren, had introduced them in 1879. When Brandeis became a justice, Holmes had already served on the Court for fifteen years.

Oliver Wendell Holmes

Brandeis considered Holmes and Taft the "only members of the Court worth talking with."[10] Brandeis loved Holmes and called him the "best intellectual machine on the Court . . . as wonderful in character as in brain."[11] None of Brandeis's likes and dislikes, however, were ever reflected in his conduct toward his colleagues on the Supreme Court. He treated those Justices who disagreed with him with respect. The phrase "Holmes and Brandeis dissenting" became famous because their dissents were in major cases that got a lot of attention. Brandeis was not usually a dissenter: 454 of his 528 opinions were written for the majority; only 74 were dissents.[12] He dissented when he thought it was important, but only after many attempts to bring the other Justices around to his way of thinking. Brandeis tried to persuade Holmes many times, and the other Justices recognized Brandeis's influence on Holmes. Talking things over with his colleagues was just one of Brandeis's techniques. When he disagreed with a majority vote or opinion, he would circulate a memo to the Court indicating that he was willing to negotiate. On some occasions, postconference thought changed Brandeis's mind about his own vote.

Oliver Wendell Holmes (middle) and Louis Dembitz Brandeis
(right) are shown here with former Chief Justice Harlan Fiske Stone
(left). Holmes and Brandeis lived about one block apart and enjoyed
taking walks together.

The Depression

The stock market began to act strangely in 1929. On October 23 there was a spectacular drop. The following day, when almost thirteen million shares changed hands, became known as "Black Thursday." Stocks reached new lows on November 13, rose slightly during the early part of 1930, but in the spring began a downward slide that hit rock bottom in the middle of 1932. Although Herbert Hoover, elected president by a landslide in 1928, said "The fundamental business of the country . . . is on a sound and prosperous basis," the Great Depression of the 1930s was in fact under way.[13] The Depression was largely responsible for the election of Franklin Delano Roosevelt in 1932.

The beginning of the Depression appeared to support Brandeis's dislike of big business. Shortly after Roosevelt's election in November 1932, he visited Brandeis's home to assure him that he would be a "progressive President."[14]

Roosevelt's "New Deal" programs aimed to achieve economic reform and individual economic security. The New Deal strengthened banks and increased the power of the Federal Reserve System. The Securities and Exchange Commission (SEC) was created to regulate stock exchanges. Social Security came into being in 1935 to provide old-age pensions for people over sixty-five. There were many recovery measures after the Depression of 1929 to place the country's economy on a solid foundation.

By 1936 the country was beginning to recover. The national income rose, and industrial production doubled. Some Republicans said that progress had been made despite the New Deal programs. Others, including many Democrats, argued that the New Deal programs had saved the country. There were still many unemployed, and many factories and

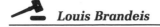

mines were still closed or working at less than full capacity. The country still faced many problems. During 1936 and 1937 Roosevelt and the New Deal supporters ran into growing difficulties. They fought back vigorously and successfully in the 1936 presidential election campaign, and Roosevelt was elected to a second term in 1937. Soon after the term began, he began his assault on certain members of the Supreme Court.

Roosevelt was unhappy that the Court had ruled as unconstitutional some important New Deal laws. He felt that members of the Court thought in old-fashioned terms, that the advanced age of the majority of the Justices kept them from thinking clearly about modern issues. On February 5, 1937, Roosevelt submitted a plan for reorganizing the Court. His idea was to appoint an extra Justice for each existing Justice who did not retire when he reached the age of seventy. In that way, the Court might be increased from its present nine members to fifteen at the most. As six of the present nine Justices were seventy or older, this proposal would have allowed Roosevelt to appoint six new Justices who would be more supportive of his New Deal programs.

Public opinion ran strongly against Roosevelt's plan. People did not want to destroy the delicate balance of legislative, executive, and judicial powers as written in the Constitution. In mid-March, the Senate Judiciary Committee held hearings on the matter. Montana senator Burton K. Wheeler, who led the campaign against Court reform, appeared before the committee and dropped a bombshell—a letter from Chief Justice Charles Evans Hughes. Hughes had replaced William Howard Taft as Chief Justice in 1930.

The letter took only a few minutes to read but came right to the heart of the matter. It showed without a doubt that the

This photo was taken with eight of the nine Supreme Court Justices in 1937—the year Roosevelt proposed his court-packing plan. Justice James Clark McReynolds is missing. Attorney General Mitchell (far left) and Solicitor General Thacher (far right) are also pictured with the Justices.

Court was keeping up with its work and that a larger Court would not be as efficient. Louis Brandeis and the other eight Justices agreed with this view. The chances for Roosevelt's Court plan to succeed were slim. He was unable to get the necessary Senate or House votes. The plan was flatly rejected.

Stepping Down from the Bench

Brandeis's physical strength began to decline in his last years on the bench. There had been consistent rumors of his retirement. But it was not until early 1939, when he was eighty-three, that he actually decided to step down. He sent a brief note to Roosevelt of his intention to retire on February 13, and Roosevelt reluctantly accepted. To Brandeis's complete satisfaction, Roosevelt named William O. Douglas to replace him on the Court. Louis Brandeis spent the last two years of his life reading, talking with friends, writing, and promoting the Zionist cause.

6

Nature Conservation and the First Amendment

Louis Brandeis felt strongly about education, free speech, and the right to privacy. Even before he became a Supreme Court Justice, he believed in the "necessity of educating both judges and the public to the connection between law and life."[1] The Supreme Court generally operates under a doctrine known as *stare decisis*, a Latin phrase meaning "let the decision stand." This doctrine provides that the principles of law established in earlier judicial decisions should be accepted as proven facts in similar later cases. However, judicial decisions are often based on historical conditions that may change as the country develops. Sometimes, a legal interpretation of the past has been made in error. New precedents may need to replace the old. Louis Brandeis did not always accept the idea of sticking to decisions of an earlier day. He would frequently quote the

Latin phrase _ex facto jus orbitur_ ("out of the facts grows the law") and declared that only when judges knew the facts could they hope to interpret a "living law." His most famous contribution to this belief was the "Brandeis Brief" of 1908. The brief in many ways changed the practice of law. Lawyers could no longer avoid the responsibility of advising the courts about relevant facts. Half a century later, in 1954, the NAACP (National Association for the Advancement of Colored People) brief detailing how segregated schools caused feelings of inferiority among African-American children played an important role in the decision in _Brown_ v. _Board of Education_, which held that segregated schools were unconstitutional.

But Brandeis's real audience lay outside the courtroom, in the public arena, the universities, and the law schools. His law clerks played a key role in his educational strategy. Their primary role was to do research and to "provide him with the facts . . . to educate bench or bar."[2] Once he had asked Dean Acheson, one of his first law clerks, to collect "footnotes covering fifteen pages."[3] In selecting a Harvard Law School graduate to serve as Brandeis's law clerk, Felix Frankfurter knew it was always preferable "to take some one whom [sic] there is reason to believe will become a law teacher."[4] Through them Brandeis knew "his message would be carried on to another generation."[5]

The First Amendment

Brandeis came to the Supreme Court when it had not yet developed a system of laws concerning the United States Constitution's First Amendment (freedom of religion, speech, and the press). He put together a more understandable

Although Brandeis (second from right, first row) spent much of his life in the courtroom—either in front of the bench or behind it—his real audience lay outside the courtroom where he could directly help people.

interpretation that has continued to be at the heart of modern First Amendment theory. The First Amendment (ratified December 15, 1791) reads:

> Congress shall make no law respecting an establishment of religion, or prohibiting the free exercise thereof, or abridging the freedom of speech, or of the press, or the right of the people peaceably to assemble, and to petition The Government for a redress of grievances.[6]

The Supreme Court in *Whitney* v. *California* found the right of an individual to associate with others who share similar beliefs to be implied within the First Amendment freedoms of speech and assembly. The Court recognized this right in 1927 when the majority upheld the conviction of social activist Anita Whitney. Whitney had violated California's "criminal syndacalism law by associating with people in an organization that advocated [supported] overthrow of the government by unlawful means."[7] Whitney never denied she was a member of the Communist Labor party, but a jury had convicted her of guilt by association.

Free Speech

Louis Brandeis wrote one of his most eloquent opinions on the value of free speech. Even though he agreed with the majority on the Court, it sounded like a dissent:

> Those who won our independence believed that the final end of the State was to make men free to develop their faculties; and that in its government the deliberative forces should prevail. . . . Recognizing the occasional tyrannies of governing majorities, they amended the Constitution so that free speech and assembly could be guaranteed.[8]

This dedication plaque at Brandeis University demonstrates that Brandeis's work will not be forgotten. As former Chief Justice Earl Warren said of Brandeis, ". . . he believed that monopoly impoverished human personality. That belief was not merely for contemplation: It was a fighting faith."

A few months after the decision was announced, Anita Whitney was pardoned by the governor of California with reasons that "echoed Brandeis's opinion."[9] Brandeis urged people to think and be fearless in speaking their minds. "There could be no liberty without courage, no happiness without liberty, and neither without the right to express themselves without fear," he said.[10]

Louis Brandeis played a key role in identifying and promoting the right to privacy. The first modern statement about this right appeared earlier in an article Brandeis and his former law partner Sam Warren published in 1890. The article grew out of Warren's annoyance at unwanted publicity. In the article Brandeis and Warren anticipated governmental and commercial intrusion into private lives, which was to become a major problem in the twentieth century. They also looked at a person's right to prevent others from using his or her name or talent for commercial reasons without prior approval. The two former law partners thoroughly researched the law on privacy. The article is considered by scholars to be the foundation for the doctrine of privacy, the "right to be let alone."[11]

Wiretap Regulation

Little more was heard of the right to privacy until the 1920s, when government officials, using new technology, listened in on other people's telephone calls. In his dissenting opinion in the 1928 case *Olmstead* v. *United States,* Brandeis vigorously protested the government's use of wiretaps. Roy Olmstead of Seattle, Washington, was convicted of transporting and selling liquor during the time when it was illegal to do so in this country. Olmstead had telephones in his office and his home.

There were also phones at the homes of his associates and at other places in the city. There was frequent communication with Vancouver, British Columbia. Times were fixed for liquor deliveries to places along Puget Sound near Seattle. From there, liquor was removed. One of the head men in the company was always on duty at the main office, where he would receive telephone orders. The telephone numbers were given to likely customers. Sometimes sales would amount to two hundred cases of liquor a day. Information about the illegal business dealings was obtained by using wiretaps. Small wires were inserted in the ordinary phone wires in the basement of the main office building. The wiretaps were made from house lines in the streets near the houses. This gathering of evidence continued for nearly five months. "Whenever a telephone line is 'tapped,'" Brandeis wrote in his dissent, "the privacy of the persons at both ends of the line is invaded. . . ."[12]

The Fourth Amendment to the Constitution provides:

> The right of the people to be secure in their persons, houses, papers, and effects, against unreasonable searches and seizures, shall not be violated, and no Warrants shall issue, but upon reasonable cause, supported by Oath or affirmation, and particularly describing the place to be searched, and the persons or things to be seized."[13]

Brandeis continued in his dissent:

> They conferred, as against the government, the right to be let alone—the most comprehensive of rights and the right most valued by civilized men. To protect that right [to be let alone] every unjustifiable intrusion by the government upon the privacy of the individual, whatever the means employed, must be deemed a violation of the Fourth Amendment."[14]

Brandeis adapted legal techniques to realities of life in the first half of the twentieth century. His legacy was the mix of "richly informed judgment and high social purpose."[15] "It is absolutely essential," he said, "in order that men may develop that they be properly fed and properly housed, and that they have proper opportunities of education and recreation. We cannot reach our goal without those things. . . ."[16]

Much of the country had changed during Brandeis's lifetime. Eighteen states had been added, and the population had increased over 400 percent. Louis Brandeis had witnessed revolutions in transportation and energy in the North, from canals and railroads to automobiles and airplanes, from wood to coal to hydroelectric power. The South and the West still remained undeveloped. In a new industrial society, it might be impossible to preserve and enjoy the forests, valleys, and waters of the West.

Nature Conservation

Brandeis was a supporter of preserving our natural resources long before it became a popular cause. Around 1910 he became involved in the Ballinger-Pinchot controversy. It involved the entire problem of conservation of the country's natural resources. President Theodore Roosevelt fought vigorously for conservation and was wholeheartedly supported by his secretary of the interior as well as the chief forester of the Department of Agriculture, Gifford Pinchot. When William Howard Taft became president in 1909, he pledged to continue Roosevelt's conservation policies. He appointed Richard A. Ballinger secretary of the interior. In August 1909, Ballinger reopened for sale certain valuable coal lands in Alaska. Brandeis did not want big enterprises to spoil the land, but he was not opposed to development of the rich land in Alaska. He told Robert LaFollette: "The people of the United States are entitled to . . . get the benefit . . . of a reduction in the cost of living . . . from the utilization of Alaska's treasures."[17]

Alaska was made up of courageous pioneers who, Brandeis thought, deserved to benefit from the fruits of their labors. Development meant expensive transportation and utility systems. The profits needed by the bankers would make development too costly for Alaskans and other Americans. Development of lands required money raised by the people.

Pinchot, who was a conservationist, accused Ballinger, who was not, of corrupting the public lands for the benefit of the bankers. Pinchot denounced Ballinger as a traitor to conservation and refused to stop his attack. Taft was forced to remove Pinchot from the Forestry Service in January 1910. A controversy developed—conservatives defended the Taft administration, the progressives charged fraud and treachery. Congress forced an investigation of the Interior Department. Louis Brandeis represented Pinchot and successfully exposed Ballinger as an opponent of conservation, someone who wanted public land distributed to private business interests. Taft continued to stubbornly defend Ballinger. Public opinion, however, was behind Pinchot due to the effective presentation of the case by Louis Brandeis, who strongly believed in individual liberties.

Zionism

It was not too big a leap for Brandeis, from conservation to Zionism. Both causes offered him the opportunity to confront big opponents, whether corporations or foreign governments.

The Balfour Declaration, drafted by British foreign minister Arthur J. Balfour and prominent Zionists, was an official statement issued in 1917 on behalf of the British government to announce its support of a proposed home for the Jewish people in Palestine. The Zionists hoped this was a promise to make Palestine a Jewish state. It was formally approved two years later in 1919, the year Louis Brandeis took his first and only trip to Palestine.

Brandeis made Zionism a cause for social justice. In the summer of 1914, he fully committed himself to the Zionist cause. To be a Jew in Palestine was to be a pioneer on the frontier. "The same spirit which brought the Pilgrim west is the spirit which has sent many a Jew to the east," Louis Brandeis said.[18]

Zionism emerged from the chaos of World War I. The British had conquered Palestine, and the Zionist dream became a reality. He wrote Alice: "It is a wonderful country . . . a miniature California, but a California endowed with all the interest which the history of man can contribute, and the deepest emotions which can stir a people."[19] A pioneering community in Israel, named after Brandeis, is called Ein Ha Shofet, meaning "Spring of the Judge."

Brandeis University

Many honors had been offered to Louis Brandeis, but he accepted only one honorary degree, from Harvard in 1891. Perhaps the best-known honor given him was the naming of a university for him. Brandeis University in Waltham, Massachusetts, was founded in 1948, seven years after Brandeis's death. President Franklin Roosevelt used to refer to Louis Brandeis as "Isaiah," after the biblical prophet. Brandeis's

On November 13, 1956, the centennial of Brandeis's birth, this
sculpture by Robert Berks was dedicated at Brandeis University in
Waltham, Massachusetts.

prophetic vision and inspiring life gave the founders of Brandeis University the inspiration to set the standards of academic excellence as their goal.

Louis Dembitz Brandeis was "a philosopher of freedom, a man who provided, for the first time in American Jurisprudence, a coherent rationale for the relationship of free expression to democratic society . . . a man who used his considerable intellectual abilities to make the law a partner in mankind's eternal seeking after liberty."[20]

Chronology

1856—Louis David Brandeis is born on November 13 in Louisville, Kentucky (changes middle name to Dembitz in 1875).

1872—Leaves with his family for three-year stay in Europe.

1873–1875—Attends Annen-Realschule, Dresden, Germany.

1875—Attends Harvard Law School, Cambridge, Massachusetts.

1877—Begins one year of graduate study at Harvard Law School.

1879—Forms law partnership with Harvard classmate Samuel D. Warren in Boston.

1889—Argues first case before United States Supreme Court.

1891—Marries Alice Goldmark in New York City.

1900—Leads fight for preservation of municipal subway systems in Boston.

1905—Argues *Lochner* v. *New York* before the Supreme Court.

1907—Through Brandeis's influence, Massachusetts Savings Bank Life Insurance bill becomes law.

1908—Argues *Muller* v. *Oregon* before the Supreme Court.

1910—Negotiates New York City Garment Workers' Strike.

1914—Becomes chairman of Executive Committee on General Zionist Affairs.

1916—Is nominated by President Wilson for Associate Justice of the United States Supreme Court; after a long Senate fight, his nomination is confirmed.

1919—Visits Palestine.

1927—Writes eloquent opinion in *Whitney* v. *California,* ruling in favor of Whitney on basis of the First Amendment.

1928—Dissents in *Olmstead* v. *United States.*

1938—*Erie Railroad Company* v. *Tompkins.*

1939—Resigns from the United States Supreme Court.

1941—Louis Dembitz Brandeis dies on October 5 in Washington, D.C.

Chapter Notes

Chapter 1

1. Elder Witt, ed., *Congressional Quarterly's Guide to the U.S. Supreme Court*, 2nd ed. (Washington, D.C.: Congressional Quarterly, 1990), p. 321.

2. Ibid.

3. *Journal of Supreme Court History* (Washington, D.C.: The Supreme Court Historical Society, 1993), p. 31.

4. *Constitution of the United States*, Amendment XIV, Section 1.

5. Alpheus T. Mason, *Brandeis: A Free Man's Life* (New York: Viking Press, 1946), p. 248.

6. Philippa Strum, *Louis D. Brandeis: Justice for the People* (Cambridge, Mass.: Harvard University Press, 1984), p. 41.

7. *Lochner* v. *New York*, 198 U.S. 45 (1905).

8. Strum, p. 119.

9. John A. Garraty, ed., *Quarrels That Have Shaped the Constitution* (New York: Harper and Row, 1964), p. 181.

10. *Journal of Supreme Court History*, p. 32.

11. Brandeis Brief, in *Muller v. Oregon*, 208 U.S. 419 (1908).

12. *Journal of Supreme Court History*, pp. 33–34.

13. Dean Acheson, *Morning and Noon* (Boston: Houghton Mifflin, 1965), p. 97.

14. Elizabeth Glendower Evans, "Justice Brandeis at Home," *Springfield Republican*, November 11, 1931, as quoted in Strum, p. 52.

15. Garraty, p. 183.

16. Ibid., p. 182.

17. Muller v. Oregon, 208 U.S. 422 (1908).

18. *Journal of Supreme Court History*, p. 32.

19. Garraty, p. 182.

Chapter 2

1. Josephine Goldmark, *Pilgrims of '48* (New Haven, Conn.: Yale University Press, 1930), p. 215.

2. *Population of the United States in 1860 from the Eighth Census* (Washington, D.C.: Superintendent of the Census, 1864).

3. Carl Sandburg, *Abraham Lincoln: The Prairie Years* (New York: Harcourt Brace, 1926), p. 449.

4. Goldmark, p. 242.

5. Alpheus T. Mason, *Brandeis, A Free Man's Life* (New York: Viking Press, 1946), p. 24.

6. Goldmark, p. 284.

7. Mason, p. 27.

8. Louis D. Brandeis, "Personal Recollections," Brandeis University Special Collections, Waltham, Mass.

9. Mason, p. 30.

10. Melvin I. Urofsky, *Louis D. Brandeis and the Progressive Tradition* (Boston: Little, Brown, 1981), p. 3.

11. Langdell, first dean of Harvard Law School, introduced the case method of instruction. Through close detailed study of cases, a student could learn the principles of law. The case method eventually replaced the lecture method during the first half of twentieth century.

12. Brandeis, "Personal Recollections."

13. Mason, p. 46.

14. Urofsky, p. 3.

15. Philippa Strum, *Louis D. Brandeis: Justice for the People* (Cambridge, Mass.: Harvard University Press, 1984), p. 30.

16. Ibid., p. 33.

17. Mason, p. 78.

Chapter 3

1. Melvin I. Urofsky, *Louis D. Brandeis and the Progressive Tradition* (Boston: Little, Brown, 1981), p. 21.

2. Philippa Strum, *Louis D. Brandeis: Justice for the People* (Cambridge, Mass.: Harvard University Press, 1984), p. 57.

3. Ibid., p. 61.

4. Brenda Marder, "Brandeis and America," *Brandeis Review*, vol. 9, no. 3 (Spring 1990), p. 16.

5. Strum, p. 78.

6. Urofsky, p. 41.

7. Marder, p. 17.

8. Strum, p. 231; Jonathan D. Sarna, "Louis D. Brandeis: Zionist Leader," *Brandeis Review* (Winter 1992), p. 22.

9. Ibid., p. 23.

10. Ibid.

Chapter 4

1. Alpheus T. Mason, *Brandeis: A Free Man's Life* (New York: Viking Press, 1946), p. 376.

2. Lewis Paul Todd and Merle Curti, *Rise of the American Nation*, vol. 2 (New York: Harcourt, Brace, 1968), p. 269.

3. Samuel Eliot Morison, *The Oxford History of the American People* (New York: Oxford University Press, 1965), p. 840.

4. Gorton Carruth, *The Encyclopedia of American Facts and Dates*, 9th ed. (New York: Harper Collins, 1993), p. 420.

5. Philippa Strum, *Louis D. Brandeis: Justice for the People* (Cambridge, Mass.: Harvard University Press, 1984), p. 207.

6. Arthur M. Schlesinger, Jr., ed., *Running for President. The Candidates and Their Images 1900–1992* (New York: Simon and Schuster, 1994), p. 85.

7. Strum, p. 292.

8. Mason, p. 466.

9. Ibid.

10. Strum, p. 292.

11. Melvin I. Urofsky, *Louis D. Brandeis and the Progressive Tradition* (Boston: Little, Brown, 1981), p. 106.

12. Ibid., p. 106.

13. Bruce Allen Murphy, *The Brandeis/Frankfurter Connection* (New York: Oxford University Press, 1982), p. 29.

14. Urofsky, p. 107.

15. Strum, p. 293.

16. Alden L. Todd, *Justice on Trial: The Case of Louis D. Brandeis* (New York: McGraw-Hill, 1964), p. 97.

17. *Boston Morning Globe*, January 31, 1916.

18. Urofsky, p. 115.

19. Mason, p. 501.

20. Ibid., p. 472.

21. Todd and Curti, p. 245.

22. Strum, p. 298.

23. "The Supreme Court on the Front Page," editorial, *The Survey*, June 10, 1916, p. 279.

Chapter 5

1. Dean Acheson, *Morning and Noon* (Boston: Houghton Mifflin, 1965), p. 51.

2. Ibid., p. 78.

3. Ibid., p. 80.

4. Bernard Schwartz, *A History of the Supreme Court* (New York: Oxford University Press, 1993), p. 215.

5. Bruce Allen Murphy, *The Brandeis/Frankfurter Connection* (New York: Oxford University Press, 1982), p. 39.

6. Ibid., p. 44.

7. *Time* (Brandeis obituary), October 13, 1941, p. 16.

8. Sheldon M. Novick, *Honorable Justice: The Life of Oliver Wendell Holmes* (Boston: Little, Brown, 1989), p. 343.

9. Catherine Drinker Bowen, *Yankee From Olympus* (Boston: Little, Brown, 1944), p. 413.

10. Philippa Strum, *Louis D. Brandeis: Justice for the People* (Cambridge, Mass.: Harvard University Press, 1984), p. 370.

11. Ibid.

12. Ibid., p. 365.

13. Gorton Carruth, *Encyclopedia of American Facts and Dates*, 9th ed. (New York: Harper Collins, 1993), p. 470.

14. Alpheus T. Mason, *Brandeis: A Free Man's Life* (New York: Viking Press, 1946), pp. 621–622.

Chapter 6

1. Melvin I. Urofsky, "Justice Louis Brandeis," in *The Jewish Justices of the Supreme Court* (Washington, D.C.: The Supreme Court Historical Society, 1994), p. 14.

2. Ibid., pp. 18–19.

3. Philippa Strum, *Louis D. Brandeis: Justice for the People* (Cambridge, Mass.: Harvard University Press, 1984), p. 355.

4. Melvin I. Urofsky, ed., *Half Brother, Half Son: The Letters of Louis D. Brandeis to Felix Frankfurter* (Norman, Okla.: University of Oklahoma Press, 1991), p. 317.

5. Urofsky, p. 19.

6. Amendment I to the Constitution of the United States, ratified December 15, 1791.

7. Elder Witt, ed., *Congressional Quarterly's Guide to the U.S. Supreme Court*, 2nd ed. (Washington, D.C.: Congressional Quarterly, 1990), p. 398.

8. *Whitney* v. *California*, 274 U.S. 377 (1927).

9. Witt, p. 402.

10. Urofsky, *The Jewish Justices of the Supreme Court*, p. 26.

11. Louis D. Brandeis and Samuel D. Warren, "The Right To Privacy," *Harvard Law Review*, Vol. 4 (1890), p. 193.

12. *Olmstead* v. *United States*, 277 U.S. 478 (1928).

13. Amendment IV to the Constitution of the United States, ratified December 15, 1791.

14. *Olmstead* v. *United States*.

15. Samuel J. Konefsky, *The Legacy of Holmes and Brandeis* (New York: Macmillan Company, 1956), p. 306.

16. Louis D. Brandeis, *The Curse of Bigness* (New York: Viking Press, 1934), p. 81.

17. Jordan A. Schwarz, *The New Dealers* (New York: Vintage/Random House, 1993), p. 117.

18. Ibid., p. 118.

19. Jonathan D. Sarna, "Louis D. Brandeis: Zionist Leader," *Brandeis Review* (Winter 1992), pp. 26 27.

20. Melvin I. Urofsky, "Louis D. Brandeis: Supreme Court Justice," *Brandeis Review* (Winter 1992), p. 13.

Where to Write

Goldfarb Library
Judaica and Special Collections Department
Brandeis University
Waltham, MA 02254
Attn: Dr. Charles Cutter, Director

Harvard Law School Library
Langdell Hall
Cambridge, MA 02138
Attn: Erika Chadbourn, Curator of Manuscripts Emerita

University Archives and Records Center
University Libraries
University of Louisville Law School
Louisville, KY 40292
Attn: Janet Hodgson, Archivist

American Jewish Historical Society
2 Thorton Road
Waltham, MA 02154

The Supreme Court Historical Society
111 Second Street, NE
Washington, DC 20002
Attn: David T. Pride, Executive Director

Glossary

amendment—A measure added to the United States Constitution since it was adopted in 1787.

anti-Semitism—Prejudice toward or dislike or hatred of Jews.

antitrust—Pertaining to rules against certain trade practices.

appeal—To take a case to a higher court.

argument—An oral presentation of a case made by an attorney.

attorney general—In the federal government, the head of the Department of Justice, appointed by the president. The attorney general is a member of the cabinet and appears on behalf of the government in all cases in which the government is interested. He or she gives legal advice to the president.

bill—A measure proposed for action before a legislative body.

Bill of Rights—The first ten amendments to the United States Constitution.

brethren—Until 1981, Supreme Court Justices were all men. They were called "brethren," which means "brothers."

brief—A written statement of essential facts including arguments and authorities in support of the position on which a lawyer seeks to persuade the court.

cabinet—A group appointed by the president to head specific executive departments and to serve as advisors.

case—A suit or some other legal action.

Chief Justice—The highest judicial officer of the United States, appointed for a life term by the president with the consent of the Senate. The Chief Justice presides over sessions of the Supreme Court.

citizen—A native or naturalized member of the United States as defined in the Fourteenth Amendment.

civil rights—Guarantees of freedoms to citizens of the United States under the United States Constitution.

conferences—Meetings where the Supreme Court Justices grant or deny judicial review and decide cases. Conferences are conducted in complete secrecy. The Chief Justice presides over the conference.

Congress of the United States—The legislative branch of the federal government consisting of the Senate and House of Representatives. Congress introduces laws, regulates commerce, coins money, establishes post offices, maintains armed forces, and declares war. The first Congress met in 1789.

Constitution of the United States—The basic law establishing the framework of government. It establishes the relationship between the people and their government. The Constitution went into effect March 4, 1789; It is the supreme law of the land.

corporation—A group of people operating, by law, as a business.

court-packing—President Franklin D. Roosevelt's proposal in 1937 to raise the number of Supreme Court Justices from nine to fifteen, to allow him to appoint new Justices who would support his New Deal programs. The plan was not enacted by Congress.

decision—The court's judgment when a case is settled.

Declaration of Independence—A basic statement of American beliefs made to declare independence of the American colonies from England. It was drafted by Thomas Jefferson, John Adams, Benjamin Franklin, Roger Sherman, and Robert Livingston and adopted on July 4, 1776.

Democratic party—One of the two major political parties in the United States. Democrats generally believe that the federal government should be actively involved in correcting social inequity. Woodrow Wilson, Franklin Delano Roosevelt, and Louis Brandeis were Democrats.

dissent—To render a minority opinion in a law case.

docket—A special calendar on which a case is scheduled.

due process—The right to fair treatment.

Electoral College—The body that officially elects the president. All electoral votes go to the candidate who wins that state. To be elected president, a candidate must win a majority of electoral votes.

First Amendment—A part of the Bill of Rights that protects freedom of speech and of the press, religious liberty, and the rights of people to assemble peacefully and to petition the government for a "redress of grievances."

Fourteenth Amendment—A part of the Constitution that defines citizenship and forbids states to deprive any person of life, liberty, or property without due process.

Fourth Amendment—A part of the Bill of Rights that prohibits "unreasonable searches and seizures."

House of Representatives—The lower house of Congress, consisting of members who represent each state. The number of representatives a state has depends on its population. A representative must be over twenty-five years old, a United States citizen for at least seven years, and a resident of the state that elects him or her. The House can impeach federal officials, originate revenue bills, and elect the president if no candidate gets a majority in the Electoral College.

immigrant—Someone who moves to a country other than their own to settle there.

judge—A government official who has the power to decide cases in a court of law. A Supreme Court government official is called a Justice.

judgment of the court—The official decision of a court based on the full review of a case. The court can uphold, modify, or reverse a decision made in a lower court. It may also void a lower-court decision. If this occurs, the court may send the case back to the lower court to be reconsidered. The court's opinion guides the lower court on the principles of law it should consider.

labor union—An organization that represents industry workers.

law clerk—A law school graduate who becomes an assistant to a judge.

lawyer—An attorney, or counsel, licensed to practice law. One who prosecutes or defends causes in federal courts or in any state. A lawyer gives legal advice in relation to any matter. He or she may do so with or without charging a fee.

minimum wage—By law, the least amount of money that a worker can be compensated.

monopoly—The exclusive control of an industry by a company or combination of companies, making it impossible or unprofitable for others to compete for a share of the market.

New Deal—A program by President Franklin D. Roosevelt during his first term in office, 1932–1936.

nonsectarian—Not limited to any particular religious denomination.

opinion—A written explanation by a judge about the legal principles on which a court decision is based.

president—The chief executive of the United States, a key official in the American system of government.

progressive—An alternative name for those who do not want to be called "liberal." The term also refers to a movement of social protest and economic reforms led by progressives. In 1912, Republicans were divided into progressives and conservatives. Theodore Roosevelt led the Progressive Movement.

Prohibition—The forbidding, by law, of transportation, manufacture, and sale of intoxicating liquors.

Republican party—The more conservative of the two major American parties. The party was organized in 1854 out of the Whig Party. Herbert Hoover, Abraham Lincoln, and William Howard Taft were Republicans.

Senate—The upper house of Congress, which has two members from each state. The Senate now has one hundred members. A senator must be over thirty years old, a United States citizen for at least nine years, and a resident of the state that elects him or her. The Senate has the power to advise and consent on appointments of important government officials, including ambassadors and federal judges.

Senate Judiciary Committee—The committee that presides over hearings on confirmation of Supreme Court Justices.

sitting—To be in session for official business.

socialist—One who supports collective or governmental ownership. Socialism is a system or condition of society in which the means of production are owned and controlled by the state.

suit—An action against a person in a court of law.

Supreme Court of the United States—The highest court in the land. It interprets the meaning of the Constitution.

term—When a court is in session.

trial—Examination by a judge with or without a jury.

unconstitutional—Not according to the wording and principles of the Constitution of the United States.

Zionist—Someone who believes in the creation of a Jewish state, a homeland for the Jews, and supports its existence. Louis Brandeis was an active Zionist.

Bibliography

Dawson, Nelson L., ed. *Brandeis & America*. Lexington, Ky.: University Press of Kentucky, 1989.

Gal, Allon. *Brandeis of Boston*. Cambridge, Mass.: Harvard University Press, 1990.

Gross, David C. *A Justice for All People*. New York: Dutton Children's Books, 1987.

Lankevich, George J., ed. *The United States Supreme Court*. vol. 1–10. Danbury, Conn.: Grolier Educational Corporation, 1995.

Patrick, John J. *The Young Oxford Companion to the Supreme Court of the United States*. New York: Oxford University Press, 1993.

Strum, Philippa. *Brandeis on Democracy*. Lawrence, KS.: University Press of Kansas, 1995.

————. *Louis D. Brandeis: Justice for the People*. Cambridge, Mass.: Harvard University Press, 1984.

Teitelbaum, Gene, ed. *Justice Louis D. Brandeis: A Bibliography of Writings and Other Materials on the Justice*. Fred B. Rothman, 1988.

Urofsky, Melvin I. *Louis D. Brandeis and the Progressive Tradition in America*. New York: HarperCollins College, 1987.

Urofsky, Melvin, ed. *The Supreme Court Justices: A Biographical Dictionary*. New York: Garland Press, 1994.

Witt, Elder, advisory ed. *The Supreme Court A to Z*. Washington, D.C.: Congressional Quarterly, 1993.

Index

New Deal, 69, 70
New Freedom, 44
New Hampshire, 26
New Haven Railroad, 37, 39
New Jersey, 36
New Republic, 52
New York, 36, 39, 62
New York Central Railroad v. *Winfield,* 62
New York Sun, 51
New York World, 52

O
Ohio, 14-16
Olmstead v. *United States,* 78
opinions, 62
Oregon Supreme Court, 6-7

P
Palestine, 82
Peckham, Rufus, 10
People's Savings Bank of Brockton, 37
Pinchot, Gifford, 80
presidential election, 45
press, 74
privacy, right to, 78-79
Progressive Movement, 33, 47

Q
Quaker City Cab Co. v. *Pennsylvania,* 62

R
radicalism, 52
railroads, 37, 39
reform movement, 33
religion, 74, 76
Roosevelt, Franklin Delano, 64, 70
Roosevelt, Theodore, 5, 44, 64

S
Saturday conference of the Court, 60
Savings Bank Life Insurance (SBLI), 36-37, 64

Securities and Exchange Commission (SEC), 69
speech, 74, 76
stare decisis, 73
state law, 62
stock market crash, 69
strike, 39, 54

T
Taft, William Howard, 44, 47, 49, 52, 66, 70
Texas, 16
Traux v. *Corrigan,* 63
trustees, 33
trusts, 33, 44

U
unions, 36, 39
United States Supreme Court, 6-7, 10, 14, 47-49, 51
University of Louisville Law School, 30

W
Warren and Brandeis, 26
Warren, Earl, 78
Warren, Samuel, 26
Washington, D.C., 8, 47, 51
West End Railway, 34
West Virginia, 49
Wheeler, Burton K., 70
White, Edward Douglas, 10, 55, 66
Whitney v. *California,* 76
Wilson, Woodrow, 42, 43-45, 64
Wisconsin, 47
workers, 36, 39, 41, 54
Works, John D., 49

Z
Zionism, 41-42, 81-82

About the Author

Suzanne Freedman is a former librarian with a penchant for biographies. Her first book concerned a civil rights activist at the turn of the century. Freedman is an involved member of her community who serves on the boards of the historical society and the scholarship fund. Her hobbies are reading, tennis, and photography.